Chasing Clouds

Adventures in a Poetry Balloon

Edited by Jonathan Humble
Illustrated by Em Humble

First published in Great Britain in 2022
by Yorkshire Times Publishing.

The copyright of the individual poems © belongs to
and remains with the contributing poets.

Copyright of the illustrations © Em Humble.

All rights reserved. No part of this publication may be reproduced, stored in or introduced into a retrieval system, or transmitted in any form or by any means (electronic, mechanical, photocopying, recording or otherwise) without prior written permission from both the publisher and the copyright owner.

ISBN: 978-1-8383227-2-4

Profits from book sales of this anthology of poems will be donated to
the National Literacy Trust
(registered charity no. 1116260).

Please be aware that a mixture of British English
and American English spellings have been used in the anthology.

Special thanks to Richard Trinder of the Yorkshire Times, Em Humble for the care and love she put into creating the illustrations and to all the lovely poets who submit their poems to the **Dirigible Balloon** for the enjoyment of our young (and old) readers.

... to see the world through poets' eyes ...

Hello Balloonists!

The **Dirigible Balloon** website features poetry written for children by both new and established poets. Our aim is to bring you some of the best work that writers for children have to offer.

We try to upload poems that will take our readers on a journey, lifting their thoughts, feelings and aspirations as though they were on an exciting flight, expanding their horizons and having lots of fun in the process.

Chasing Clouds is our first anthology, chosen from over 500 poems. It couldn't have been published without the kind permission and support of our brilliant poets and the encouragement of the lovely people at the **Yorkshire Times**.

The profit made from the sales of this book will be donated to **The National Literacy Trust**, an independent charity dedicated to developing the literacy skills that disadvantaged children need to succeed.

We hope you enjoy the poems.

Jonathan Humble
Editor of The Dirigible Balloon

Suppose we were not here today
but on adventures far away.

Within a bright hot air balloon
we'd skim the clouds beneath the moon,

traverse the seas, touch mountain peaks
and fly with birds for many weeks.

We'd visit places fine and rare
with splendid views beyond compare.

Our thoughts cut loose, we'd search the skies
to see the world through poets' eyes

then tell our friends where we had been
and talk and sing of all we'd seen.

Contents

How to Conjure a Poem in Eight Easy Steps 1
Julie Anna Douglas

A Poem is Like a Balloon 2
Philip Ardagh

Recipe For Flying 3
Julie Stevens

Head in the Clouds 4
Charlie Bown

River Morning Walk 6
A.F. Harrold

Ballerina Cherry Tree 7
Stephanie Henson

Suitcase Poem 8
Michael Rosen

Tell it to the Bees 10
Carole Bromley

A Family Song 11
Dean Flowerfield

One of the Dogs I Don't Have 12
Rob Walton

My Dog is a Three-Letter Spell 13
Annick Yerem

What the Cat Knows 14
Attie Lime

The Wrong Way Round 16
Zaro Weil

The Octopus Tango 18
Moe Phillips

Floordrobe 20
Jacqueline Shirtliff

Ghost in the Machine 21
   Lesley James

You See 21
   Fiona Halliday

World Muck Day 22
   Rob Walton

Think Of It 24
   Zaro Weil

Moon Morning 25
   Carol Coven Grannick

What the City Pigeon Hears 26
   Emma Purshouse

A Sticky Toffee Poem 27
   Helen Dineen

Down-a-down-Derry 28
   Jane Lovell

Earwig Corner 30
   Brian Moses

Hugs and Ladybugs 31
   Jacoby Crane

Belinda Bean the Bouncing Queen 32
   Colin West

Mum Taught You That 33
   Charlie Bown

New School Shoes 34
   Sarah Ziman

The Boy Who Left His Bum Behind 35
   Colin West

Spelling Test 36
   Fi Calvert

We Girls 37
   Nina Parmenter

What are Little Girls Made Of ? 38
   Piu DasGupta

Cauld Kail an Custard 40
  David Bleiman

Cakey Yum Yum 41
  Nina Parmenter

Pop the Ferret! 42
  Jane Lovell

Granny and Grandad 43
  Sarah Ziman

What I Love About Jazz 44
  Stewart Ennis

Scotch Bonnet 45
  Elizabeth McGeown

Disco Bumblebee 46
  Dale Neal

Happiness Is 47
  Kay Medway

Dance of the Stream Sprite 48
  Jacqueline Shirtliff

Stones on the Beach 49
  Helen Openshaw

The Water Cycle 50
  Brian Mackenwells

Daytime's Story 51
  Gaynor Andrews

Earth Day 52
  Philip Ardagh

Moth 52
  Daniel Page

A Skyfall of Verbs 53
  Val Harris

Cutie Fruitie 54
  Gaynor Andrews

Caution! This Poem Will Make You Yawn! 55
    Attie Lime

Look What I've Found 56
    David Webb

Spring's Magic Wings 57
    Linda Middleton

Elastic Days 58
    Paula Thompson

Recess Rules 59
    Helen Kemp Zax

Wet Play 60
    Fi Calvert

Sonnet Moon 62
    Debra Bertulis

Sia Jumping 63
    Chrissie Gittins

Shell 64
    Paula Thompson

Sandy Days 65
    Clara McShane

Mermaid 66
    Sarah Wallis

Bedtime 67
    Coral Rumble

Help Line 68
    Brian Mackenwells

Elliot's Laces 70
    Elenore Byrne

Fun Friday 70
    Fiona Halliday

I Cry 71
    Jonathan Sellars

Secret Toenail Clipper 71
  Alex Price

A Rainy Day 72
  Rhiannon Oliver

Storm Coming 73
  Gillian Spiller

Window Holiday 74
  Catherine Olver

At Sunrise 75
  Kathryn Dove

Balloons on Sticks at Parties: why we are all a bit cross 76
  Lesley James

The Magic 78
  Lisa Varchol Perron

I Wish 79
  Tom Moody

Advice for Meeting a Yeti 80
  Coral Rumble

A Hug for your Head 81
  Carl Burkitt

Magic in the Air 82
  Elisabeth Kelly

Wintertime Fair 83
  Mary E. Cronin

Winter Fairies 84
  Moe Phillips

Christmas Sounds 86
  Carole Bromley

The Snowman's List 87
  Julie Anna Douglas

Home Sweet Home 88
  Nannie Shakespeare

The Gift 89
  Helen Dineen

How to Conjure a Poem in Eight Easy Steps
Julie Anna Douglas

1. Take a magical pen carved from the bark of the Everbronze Tree and forged in Phoenix flames.
2. Dip in the mystical ink of the deepest, darkest depths of the Octopus Ocean.
3. Weave invisible parchment from delicate threads of moon dust, sunbeams, snowflakes and unicorn tears.
4. Sprinkle with the essence of luck from the pot of gold at the end of a triple rainbow.
5. Travel by paper aeroplane to the lost island of Alonio and build yourself a writing hut from the leaves of the lesser-spotted Peek-a-Boo Plant.
6. Contemplate for a century, dream for a decade and wonder for a week.
7. Write in perfect time to the rhythm of a resting dragon's heartbeat.
8. Wrap your completed poem in cloud-silk, spun by the seven silver, singing, sprite sisters of the southern skies and post to the universe on a first class shooting star.

A Poem is Like a Balloon
Philip Ardagh

A poem is like a balloon,
he said.
It starts off small
and grows and grows,
he said.
And then, like all good ideas, takes flight,
making us marvel and look in wonder,
he said.
He said that a poem is like a balloon.

Recipe For Flying
Julie Stevens

I've jewels in this bag I carry with me
my collection will give you wings,
the shimmer of a star
the leap of a hare,
this is where magic begins.

I sneak outside, quiet as pure air
catch them as they lie low,
the wisp of a cloud
the pearl of sound,
nestled in my bag as I go.

The sway of a leaf, the warmth of sun's hand
a petal that glows with ease,
the swirl of a river
a hidden whisper,
I gather them all to please.

Come take a look, see what lies within
listen to the singing inside,
lift your arms and
believe these charms,
pretty soon your feet will rise.

Head in the Clouds
Charlie Bown

Teacher says,
Get your head out,
Right out,
Out of the clouds.

Nothing good can come
From having a head
Stuck in the clouds,
He says.

Before I take my head
Out of the clouds
I look around,
Around at the clouds.

And I see magicians
Explorers
Adventurers
Artists
And dancers.
I see movers
And makers
Singers
Wakers
Dreaming.

In the clouds
I see mysteries for solving
Stories for telling
Challenges for taking
Lives for saving
Questions for wondering
And my head
In the clouds,

Exactly where it belongs.

River Morning Walk
A.F. Harrold

Bright spikes of sun
splinter across the river-top –
rippling light that tickles my eyes
like soft-fingered glass.

In the tree a robin watches,
orange breast turned away,
black bead eye turned my way.
For a time neither of us move.

The sky's an ocean
you can't see the bottom of.
It's blue all the way up, today.
All the way.

Ballerina Cherry Tree
Stephanie Henson

A grand Weeping Cherry Tree sways,
Tall in stature, a presence in and of itself -
Long lines extend into the world around it.
Arched branches mimic ballerina feet,
Elegantly stretch down to the ground.
Vivid leaves dance effortlessly with flow.
The feel of tutu petals spinning in the wind,
Often backstage to more vibrant stars -
Green at first, on point to bloom.
Thus, once a year - a chance to shine.
Company of pure pink petals flourish,
Pirouette & Jete around the surface.
To the beat of seasons changing,
Nature's choreography dazzles.
A position to transform,
Velvet beauty of rebirth.

Suitcase Poem
Michael Rosen

I'm a suitcase
in the attic all year
I'm a suitcase
stuffed full of gear
I'm a suitcase
crammed in a hold
I'm a suitcase
freezing cold.

Well yes ...

I may be a suitcase
but I want to be free
I want to go to the beach
and swim in the sea
I want to go to the mountains
and learn how to ski
I want to hear music
dance and shout
You leave me in the room
when you go out.
But I don't want to be baggage
It's not what I want to be.
I'm a suitcase
and I want to be free.

Next trip you take
you're in for a shock
I may be quiet
shut tight with a lock
But while you're out
enjoying the sun
I'll escape
I'll be on the run
A suitcase on the move
looking for fun.
I'll be that suitcase
Yes, that'll be me
I'm a suitcase
who wants to be free.

Tell it to the Bees
Carole Bromley

Honeybee, honeybee on my flower
will you be here in half an hour?

Honeybee, honeybee on the tree
what will you tell your friends about me?

Honeybee, honeybee fuss and buzz
what will you say to the hive about us?

Honeybee, honeybee movement not sound
tells the others where flowers are found.

Honeybee, honeybee's wiggling dance
could have them all flying to Spain or France.

Honeybee, honeybee don't tell them please -
I am a little bit frightened of bees!

A Family Song
Dean Flowerfield

My father is a giant,
my Ma a tiny elf.
My sister is a fairy queen
but me, I'm just myself.

My Granny is a jumping jack,
my Gramps a Christmas tree.
My brother is a big balloon
but I, well I'm just me.

My uncle is an ice cream cone,
my aunt a mincemeat pie.
My cousins all are candy canes
and me, well I'm just I.

I've got a funny family,
they're quite a sight to see.
For each is strange or silly
but I, well I'm just me.

One of the Dogs I Don't Have
Rob Walton

One of the dogs I don't have
has left dirty marks
all over the front door.
I think it was the brown Poodle with the innocent eyes.

One of the dogs I don't have
has knocked a vase of flowers
all over the kitchen floor.
I think it was the black Labrador with the velvet collar.

One of the dogs I don't have
has woken my mum
with the world's loudest snore.
I think it was the Jack Russell with the wispy beard.

One of the dogs I don't have
has taken the crisps
out of the secret drawer.
I think it was the Border Collie who likes Eastenders.

One of the dogs I don't have
has said I need that dog
I'm always asking for.
I think it could have been any
one of the dogs I don't have.

My Dog is a Three-Letter Spell
Annick Yerem

faith turned fur, an incantation. I am sure he can fly, especially at night, across rabbit-blooming fields, across pasta valleys, over tripe rivers, sausage mountains. He can hear mice dreaming, he is one step ahead, then ten.

My dog is a prayer, all ears, all joy, all yes. When it's hot, it's hot, when it's cold it's cold. Food is love is being there is breathing. The world does not have to be complicated.

My place in his heart is at least as wide and loud as the fridge door opening.

My dog is this moment, is present, is a lesson in here.

He owes me nothing. I owe him cheese. I owe him joy.

What the Cat Knows
Attie Lime

Mum's tall spotty jug isn't tall anymore
it's in hundreds of pieces all over the floor
I rocked it and knocked it as I ran through the door
Mum thinks it was me, but she isn't sure.
(The cat knows I did it.)

The jug was the prettiest thing in the hall
Mum loved it because it was bright and tall
I'm neither of those – I'm quite dull and small
I really didn't mean to make it fall.
(The cat knows I did it.)

Mum found me crouching, trying to sweep
she shouted then began to weep
"My jug!" she wailed, "It wasn't cheap!"
that night I couldn't get to sleep.
(The cat knows I did it.)

I told Mum about the hairs on the mat
which match the colour of our cat
she frowned and said "Well, fancy that!"
the cat stayed silent where he sat.
(The cat knows I did it.)

Mum asked me outright "Was it you?"
my fingers shook, my blood turned blue
I hate to lie, that much is true
I said the cat hair was a clue.
(The cat knows I did it.)

My cat used to sleep upon my bed
he nuzzled love all round my head
now he glares as if he wants me dead
"I should have told the truth," I said.
(The cat knows I did it.)

The Wrong Way Round
Zaro Weil

sitting
the wrong way round in the train
can't help but notice
I am heading backwards through today

cause from my speeding
window-blur
outside fades away
erasing most things
soon minutes vanish
hours dissolve
years hurtle past
then centuries
then ages

world grows younger
and earlier
and earlier
mature trees now saplings
distant mountains shrink to ancient flat-lands
great whales walk the earth
starlings become packs of low-swooping dinosaurs

I hurtle backwards
even faster
past last spring
and the winter before that
past my parents
my ancestors
my clan
my species

the rest of living things

until I am an atom
like every other atom
as old and new
as fiery and uncertain

as the fuzzy beginning of us all
never knowing
let alone dreaming

that one day
I would be me
seated on a train traveling
the wrong way round

The Octopus Tango
Moe Phillips

Down in the depths on the ocean floor
lies an old sea cave with a wooden door.
This cold and cavernous, watery hall
is home to the Octopus Tango Ball.

Hidden away in this abysmal deep,
mollusks master their "Barada Sweep"!
In the dim, dank hall, they take their places,
tentacles tangle in tango embraces.

A dim chandelier from a sunken ship,
sways in the waves as the cave walls drip.
The maestro signals: the dance must begin!
The eight-legged partners start to spin.

A scarlet octopus stamps her heels.
Her blue-ringed partner slithers and kneels.
She dangles a ruby rose in her beak,
brushes its thorn against his cheek.

Their colors change as they swirl and slink.
Not spilling so much as a drop of ink.
Those boneless bodies never go slack
As they do the "Ocho", forward and back.

Round suckers pucker with every move
As the musicians play a Tango groove.
In murky waters, the dance marches on
At the Octopus Tango Marathon.

Floordrobe
Jacqueline Shirtliff

Why use a wardrobe?
The carpet works fine!
Why waste your cash
On a box made of pine?
Not got enough dresses?
Just buy a few more!
There's no limit to what
You can fit on the floor.
Don't spend precious time
Putting clothing away
When there's just so much more
You can do with your day.
Yes, my bedroom's a tip,
I have to agree,
'Cause my wardrobe's a floordrobe,
But that's fine by me!

Ghost in the Machine
Lesley James

I am the avatar of alliteration
The ghastly geist of ghoulish memes
The Tik-Tok tactic of anticipation
The silent stalker of suspicious zines

I am the Zen denizen of Zoom
The deadly double-click of doom
The hapless horror, haunting all your screens …
I am the ghost in the machine.

You See
Fiona Halliday

I see dark clouds gather overhead
You see a giant's blanket for his bed
I see a sink full of dishes to be done
You see bubbles and endless fun
I see a cupboard full of all our clutter
You see Aladdin's cave and wishes flutter
I see a carpet with toys over-strewn
You see adventure for a whole afternoon
All grownups could learn a thing or two
From looking at the world like children do!

World Muck Day
Rob Walton

Today is a very special day.
Muck and muckiness will be celebrated
in schools and homes and libraries
in countries across the world.

Muck will be delivered to classrooms
along with special muck vouchers
that children can exchange
for dirt, mud and filth.

Teachers will bring muck into school
and all will dress up as mucky characters
like The Paper Bag Princess,
Stig of the Dump or Harry the Dirty Dog.

Parents will be in a last-minute rush
to find enough muck in the mucky supermarkets
to smear all over their mucky children
before combing their mucky hair and taking them to
mucky school.

Muckshelves and muckcases will groan
under the weight of new muck
and all will be excited to find out about
the Muck of the Week.

It's not just a day for muckworms.
All children will design muck covers and write muck reviews.
At the end of the day we will all go home
and cuddle up with our favourite muck.

Happy World Muck Day!

Think Of It
Zaro Weil

think of it

the first shudder of damp
somehow signalled
all was ready
then in the deep inside of earth
in the muted underneath of winter
spring began

not with a sudden trumpet of green
or a sky of confetti blossoms
but with a seed
small, pale and barely breathing

it lay quietly
waiting for the lavender clouds
that carry the first warm rains
till for some reason as ancient and
everyday as the sun itself

the seed cracked
split and softly burst into
a faint tendril
a root a sprout
a thin wisp of a growing thing

and with no thought of stopping
it pushed through the
dark soil with the force of
a billion winter winds
until it

pierced the crust of the outside and
split the frozen armour of earth
which has held spring safe
since time began

Moon Morning
Carol Coven Grannick

Early morning silent walk
and moon beckons us
desiring attention, dressing herself
in silky clouds,
swirling like saris
draping her in softness,
ending her night time dance.

What the City Pigeon Hears
Emma Purshouse

night falling
the easing of brickwork
the settling of slates
the rumble of trains
formation of stalactites
under the arches

the whisper of feathers
the stiffening of trees
a phone ringing in an empty office
earth worms tunnelling
splish of water in the fountains
and the rats in their thousands
squeaking of sewerage
deep underground

A Sticky Toffee Poem
Helen Dineen

Sticky fingers, sticky thumbs,
(Got a toffee from my mum.)

Sticky lips and sticky chin,
(Pop the wrapper in the bin.)

Sticky nose and sticky cheeks,
(Might be chewing it for weeks.)

Sticky ears and sticky hair,
(Can't believe it got up there.)

Sticky pets and sticky friends,
(Who knows where this story ends?)

Eating toffees can be tricky,
when they make you SUPER-STICKY!

Down-a-down-Derry
Jane Lovell

Will you show me the paths that the foxes use
when all but the moon is asleep,
the rustling grass of the midnight fields
where the brown-eyed field-mice peep?

Will you tell me the secrets told by the breeze
as she wanders the woods by night,
the whispers of leaves as she moves through the trees
setting the moths to flight?

Will you take my hand and lead me where
the wood nymphs cast their dreams,
the foxglove glades where the oak tree shades
their dance from the moon's soft gleam?

Will you magic me small so I can crawl
through the hole in the wall to play,
and leave me there with the wild wee folk
till the sun lights up the day?

Will you never tell of the secret dell
where the faerie laughter rings,
or the empty bed I've left behind
till the early blackbird sings?

Oh I'll take you where the faeries play
in the midnight moonlit trees
but you'll never return to the land of men
and you'll never sleep tight in your bed again
and all you can do if you miss your friends
is whisper their names on the breeze.

Earwig Corner
(name given to a road junction near Lewes in East Sussex)

Brian Moses

Think I've discovered
What happens round
Earwig Corner.

It's always a crush, earwigs in a rush,
Giving each other the brush off
Round Earwig Corner.

A scurry of earwigs,
Always in a hurry
Round Earwig Corner.

Schemers, dreamers, freedom fighters,
A football team - Earwigs United
Round Earwig Corner.

A blur, a flash, a dash of earwig,
A smash & grab raid, a parade
Round Earwig Corner.

Earwigs doing earwiggy things,
Zipping between the fauna & flora
Round Earwig Corner.

And earwigs too
Have taken over this poem,
You'll notice an earwig bonanza
In every stanza.

Hugs and Ladybugs
Jacoby Crane

If you're having a dreary day,
And feeling a little blue,
Think of hugs & ladybugs,
You'll feel better; it's true!

You may not feel good enough,
But trust me, yes you are,
You can have my hugs & ladybugs,
Keep on shining little star!

Ignore those pesky pesty doubts,
That whisper in your ear,
Hush them with hugs & ladybugs,
Show them you have no fear!

So keep on smiling, do not fret,
This is where you belong,
With all of the hugs & ladybugs,
You are brave and strong!

Belinda Bean the Bouncing Queen
Colin West

Belinda Bean, the Bouncing Queen,
The most amazing act you've seen:
She bounces low, she bounces high,
She bounces where the birdies fly,
She bounces up, she bounces down,
She bounces over all the town,
She bounces night, she bounces noon,
She bounces half way to the moon.
Belinda Bean, the Bouncing Queen,
Can't wait to get a trampoline!

Mum Taught You That
Charlie Bown

Jump on the sofa,
Dive off the bed,
Make a den of blankets,
Wear knickers on your head.

Blow bubbles in your milk,
Jump out and shout BOO!
Launch into puddles,
Put jelly in your shoe.

Dance around the kitchen,
Put bananas in your hat.
And if anyone asks why,
Say your mum taught you that.

New School Shoes
Sarah Ziman

Box fresh but they're total nasties
Kind of look like Cornish pasties
Why can't Mum see these are ghastly –

NEW SCHOOL SHOES?

Know they'll turn my toes to mincemeat
Rather wear boots made of concrete
Like two cruise ships steering my feet –

NEW SCHOOL SHOES

Made to walk around the shop floor
Clomping like an angry centaur
These kicks are a TOTAL eyesore –

NEW SCHOOL SHOES

Street cred killed dead as the dodo
Shunned like poor old Quasimodo
Boring and safe as a Volvo –

NEW SCHOOL SHOES

No way I'll be winning races
Tripping over too-long laces
Well OF COURSE I'm pulling faces –

NEW SCHOOL SHOES!

The Boy Who Left His Bum Behind
Colin West

No wonder Hugh is looking glum,
The poor boy has mislaid his bum:
Upon a double decker bus
He travelled like a lot of us,
But when he got off at his stop
He'd left his bottom on the top.

Now Hugh has lost his derrière,
It's disappeared to Who-knows-where.
So if the bum you chance to see,
Please hand in to Lost Property,
And meanwhile always bear in mind —
Don't leave behind your own behind!

Spelling Test
Fi Calvert

My score out of ten was a piddly two
cos the teacher said 'toilet' and I wrote down 'loo'.
When she called out 'peculiar', I jotted down 'odd'.
When she said, "Write down poke, please." I noted down 'prod'.

My teacher looked over it later and said
(whilst looking confused and scratching her head),
"I don't understand it, this test is absurd!
Why not just write down the words that you heard?"

"I couldn't spell those, so I wrote some I could.
They mean the same thing, are they not just as good?"
She said that they weren't and that, on the next test,
I should try a bit harder, at least have a guess.

Well, I tried that the next week and got them all wrong!
My brain and right-spellings just don't get along.
In future, I'll stick to the way I know best
and just write down words I can spell in a test.

We Girls
Nina Parmenter

Each daisy's a piece of the moon
strewn on the welcoming grass,
waiting for fidgeting fingers to pass
and weave it in bangles and bows.
Those are not alleys, they're dens -
we seize them, we lose them, we take them again,
and dance as our dynasties grow.
Pavements and bollards and walls
are obstacle courses that shift as they call;
hop-trip with our quickstepping feet.
Sweet is the lure of the slopes,
as laughing we log-roll and slip-slide and hope
to emerge with our kneecaps complete.
Meetings in hedge-huddled homes,
stones which are amulets,
sticks which are witchety wands,
bonds that we build as we talk,
chalking graffiti and hopscotch wherever we walk.
Home with the set of the sun,
running, at one with the fun of our world ...
We girls sing to a time-honoured tune –
each daisy's a piece of the moon.

What are Little Girls Made Of ?
Piu DasGupta

What are little girls made of?
What are little girls made of?
Swords and roars and dinosaurs
pirates, Death Stars, dragons' claws
castles, pistols, ragged shirts
bows and arrows, finger-dirt
grubby knees and paint-stained faces
every lack of social graces.
That's what little girls are made of.

What are little boys made of?
What are little boys made of?
Ribbons, bows, curly locks
Lady Gaga, sparkly socks
fluffy diaries, friendship bracelets
secret notes in hidden places
cupcakes topped with chocolate sprinkles
fairy wands that wink and twinkle.
That's what little boys are made of.

But, you say, hang on a mo –
I am a pirate with a bow.
Or actually, I'd rather be
making cupcakes up a tree.
No, I'm a princess with a patch -
Don't stress, it's fine to mix and match.
By far the best is to be true
to the bestest person: YOU.

Cauld Kail an Custard
David Bleiman

Cauld kail an custard,
Grannie's awfie flustered;
stovies noo, in bramble stew,
dinna ken whit A can do;
A'm fit tae boak, A'm no that weel,
she's bilin mince wi aipple peel;
tatties next, champit in jeelie -

"Haud yer weesht, she's ninety-three!"

A Glossary of Scottish Words:

kail - cabbage
awfie - rather
stovies - potatoes baked with leftover scraps of meat and gravy
bramble - blackberry
dinna ken - don't know
fit tae boak - feeling nauseous
tatties - potatoes
champit - mashed
jeelie - jam
haud yer weesht - shut up

Cakey Yum Yum
Nina Parmenter

One lost pea on a cinnamon tree
Two giggle-bunnies on a hill (Hee hee)
Three French fish in a factory
And a slice of cake for me! (Yum yum)

Four small boys singing baba-doo-dee
Five little bites from a flea (What flea?)
Six grains of sand playing chicken with the sea
And a slice of cake for me! (Yum yum)

Seven posh pigs strutting stylishly
Eight awful aunts on a bus (Coo-ee!)
Nine black holes – oh, catastrophe!
And a slice of cake for me! (Yum yum)

"What ho!" says the vicar, "Will you have another slice?"
"Ooh YES," I reply, "how nice." (Yum yum)

Pop the Ferret!
Jane Lovell

Mr Baker had a ferret.
He used to feed it corn and millet,
crackers, nuts and bits of chocolate,
honey puffs straight from the packet,
on a Friday, salmon fillet,
Sunday lunch, a piece of brisket,
bedtimes, half a chocolate biscuit
(he liked to watch the ferret nibble it).
Summer evenings, watching cricket,
he tucked it safely in his jacket,
fed it lumps of pomegranate.
Once he thought he'd gone and lost it,
found it in a cornflake packet.
The box was empty, Ferret ate it.

Mr Baker had a ferret
Did he call it Fred, or Hubert,
Simon, Geoff or maybe Robert,
Nipper, Ripper, Jaws or Albert?
No.
He called it POP!!

Granny and Grandad
Sarah Ziman

Make-believer
Ouch-reliever
Jam-maker
Cake-baker
Book-reader
Garden-weeder
Veg-grower
Hug-bestower
Bird-spotter
List-jotter
Coffee-drinker
Sunshine-thinker
World-explorer

Cap-wearer
Poem-sharer
Shopping-fetcher
Sofa-stretcher
Campfire-lighter
Story-writer
Quiz-winner
Wide-grinner
Kite-flyer
Paper-buyer
Glasses-loser
Armchair-snoozer
Loud-snorer

Me-adorer!

What I Love About Jazz
Stewart Ennis

I love its cool piz**azz**,

its swingin' ra**z**amatazz.

The way it's not locked up like **A**lcatraz.
      The way it lies on the couch,
      its lazy shuffle and slouch,

      I love its witchy fingers and its **feline** crouch.

I love its **high** hat.

I love its **black** cat.

I love its boogie **woogie**, and its **rat** a tat tat.

      I love its **midnight** blues

      and all its **mournful** hues,

      I love its be- bop **bounce**, its bossa-nova **ooze**.

I love those ja**zz** bands

I love those ja**zz** hands
I love all that jazz

      I love ... All ... **That** ... **Jazz.**

Scotch Bonnet
Elizabeth McGeown

Scotch Bonnet! Scotch Bonnet!
Is the hottest of the chillies.
Scotch Bonnet! Scotch Bonnet!
Because my Dad is super silly.
Scotch Bonnet! Scotch Bonnet!
Tried to eat one for his tea.
Scotch Bonnet! Scotch Bonnet!
Resulting in hilarity.
Scotch Bonnet! Scotch Bonnet!
His eyes bulged out, his face turned red.
Scotch Bonnet! Scotch Bonnet!
'He looks all sunburnt!' Mummy said.
Scotch Bonnet! Scotch Bonnet!
He drank two pints of semi-skimmed.
Scotch Bonnet! Scotch Bonnet!
Produced unearthly-sounding wind.
Scotch Bonnet! Scotch Bonnet!
I sat back laughing in my chair.
Scotch Bonnet! Scotch Bonnet!
Cos it was me that made the dare!

Disco Bumblebee
Dale Neal

Busy in the summer breeze,
bags of pollen in his knees,
gets through gallons of Frizz-Ease
Disco Bumblebee

Loves his old Bee Gees LPs,
all the other bees think he's
a species from the seventies
Disco Bumblebee

Hair so big it's quite unreal,
like a wig to touch and feel,
really digs the cuban heel
Disco Bumblebee

Listens to old disco tracks,
collecting pollen in his sacks,
gold medallion round his thorax
Disco Bumblebee

When he lands inside the hive
he does a funky waggle jive,
"Ah .. ha .. ha .. ha .. stayin' alive, stayin' alive!"
Disco Bumblebee

Busy in the summer breeze,
bags of pollen in his knees,
really pleased to be one, he's
a Disco Bumblebee

Happiness Is
Kay Medway

Sometimes your happiness is a stationery shop.
Inviting, creative and colourful, like a shiny new box of
colour pencils opened on Christmas or New Year's Eve: how
will you choose only one favourite, from the shop shelves
filled with creative jewels and gems, artistic dreams and
excitement, when you forget your every worry as you begin
to window-shop?
Other times it is mum's spider plant, a glimpse
of precious happiness in green, a burst of her cares and
promises.
But yesterday, it was the jingle of mum's voice to tell us her
house plants' names in songs of family and flowers.

(Poem after Jack Underwood)

Dance of the Stream Sprite
Jacqueline Shirtliff

Shuffle through the shady shallows,
Leap from log to log,
Tango past the tangled brambles,
Tiptoe round the bog.

Skipping, stepping, pirouetting where the minnows teem;
I'm dancing to the mesmerizing music of the stream.

Balance over broken branches,
Limbo under bridges,
Twist and turn through murky tunnels,
Samba with the midges.

Skipping, stepping, pirouetting where the minnows teem;
I'm dancing to the mesmerizing music of the stream.

Waltz wildly down the waterfalls,
Gallop up the glen,
Slip smoothly through deep glassy pools
Then dance it all again!

Skipping, stepping, pirouetting where the minnows teem;
Come, join me in my dancing to the music of the stream.

Stones on the Beach
Helen Openshaw

The beach is like a library,
Come and pick a stone.
Each one tells a story,
Which one would you like to hear?
The sea is calling us to stop,
And hold a stone in our hand,
To feel its weight and shape.
Just look!
For a minute the world is a painting,
there in the palm of your hand,
And we can tell stories together,
of lands far away, forever.

The Water Cycle
Brian Mackenwells

As the rain breaks and falls,
the stones wake up
and shake the earth
from themselves.
They stretch,
but do not feel the benefit.
Each one a map
of craters and cracks,
their roughness carved
by glaciers now long gone.
They gaze up
to see if they can spot
a drop they know
from those solid
beginnings.
But the rain
has no time to catch up,
it has a world to shape,
and so the rocks
settle
again
to
sleep.

Daytime's Story
Gaynor Andrews

Daybreak glows,
Pink and rose.
Morning new,
Sky stretched blue,
Yellow rays, golden days.
Plips and plops, silver drops.
Purple shadows gently play,
Daylight hours slip away.
Red and orange sunset glory
Softly closes daytime's story.
Grey shades, colour fades.
Evening falls,
Black calls.

Earth Day
Philip Ardagh

The ground beneath our feet
The soil between our fingers
The air we breathe
The wind that blows
The rains that falls
The rivers that run
The trees that blossom
The birds that sing from their branches
Earth our home
It cares for us
As we should care for it

Moth
Daniel Page

From powdered wing, to lunar sky
She makes her way, from shadowed place
With longing heart and moon shot eye
From powdered wing, to lunar sky
The trickster moon, brings silent sigh
From muted orbs of ashen face
From powdered wing, to lunar sky
She makes her way, from shadowed place

A Skyfall of Verbs
Val Harris

I hear the sound of a whirl of birds
As they weave and dive
And shimmer and swirl.

I see the lift of a gust of leaves
As they fly with the wind
And twist and twirl.

I smell the sky in an autumn fire
As it smokes and wraps
Where the swept leaves lie.

I feel the air around my head,
The breath of the wind
And its drawn-out sigh.

Cutie Fruitie
Gaynor Andrews

Apricots are tasty,
Apples have a crunch,
I'm the cutie-fruitie.
I'm the sweetest of the bunch.

Oranges are orange,
Blueberries are blue.
I'm a ruby-fruitie
And delicious through and through.

Blackberries in hedges
Pick them if you please.
I'm a cutie-beauty
And I dangle from the trees.

Have you guessed me yet?
Ripened by the sun,
I'm a juicy-fruitie
And I'm loved by everyone.

Queen of springtime blossom,
Cream of any crop.
Truly cutie-fruitie,
I'm the CHERRY on the top.

Caution! This Poem Will Make You Yawn!
Attie Lime

I get a feeling in my mouth
it starts just like an itch
then it spreads out to my cheeks
and begins to make them twitch.
The sensation comes at bedtime
and sometimes in the morning
I can tell it's starting up again
yes - I'm very nearly Y A W N I N G!
I'll try to hold it in my mouth
perhaps no-one can see
that behind my teeth I'm bursting
to set a big one free.
I must look like I'm chewing
or I really need the loo
my face is stretched and fit to pop
does it happen to you, too?

Look What I've Found
David Webb

Look what I've found
Inside this apple core.
Little dark, shiny seeds,
Two or three, or more.
I'll plant them in the garden
In amongst the weeds.
I'll water them and care for them,
I love my little seeds.

Tiny shoots will start to grow
And sprout fresh green leaves.
Taller, stronger, reaching up
Until they're sturdy trees.
Rosy red apples,
To pick on Autumn days.
Sweet and crisp and juicy,
Ripened by sun's rays.

Look what I've found
Inside this apple core.
Little dark, shiny seeds,
Miracles for sure!

Spring's Magic Wings
Linda Middleton

Bluebells are ringing, birds are sweet singing
Across the swaying sea.
Sleek adders are snaking, trees are waking,
Feeling long-winter-free.
Butterflies are twirling, blossom is swirling
In the lemony light.
Streams are tinkling, anemones are twinkling
Star-dusted from the night.
Frogs are leaping, pollen veils are sweeping
In the playful breeze.
Leaves are unfurling, silk threads are whirling –
Caterpillar trapeze!
Woodpeckers are drumming, bees are humming,
Finding their zest and zing.
Cuckoos are deceiving, swallows are weaving –
Spring's found its magic wings!

Elastic Days
Paula Thompson

Elastic days,
brimming with promise.
School bags gather dust
while we gather possibilities
and string them, jewel-like,
across six weeks.
Net curtains billow,
ushering rose-petal breezes;
summer drifting in
to beckon us out.
Grass cuttings and grazed knees.
My bike,
no longer a wheeled thing
but a living, breathing creature
with mane and tail.
We gallop to the park,
my sister and me.
Free
to do anything
and nothing.
We lie on our backs,
grass prickling our legs,
heads craned to the sky.
And the whole world tilts.
This never-ending summer.

Recess Rules
Helen Kemp Zax

Rip the skin off both knees when you slide into first.

Exercise in the sun till you're dying of thirst.

Clown around till your teacher warns, "Stop now. Too much."

Earn a bruise on your butt when you jump Double Dutch.

Spin wild circles so crazy your stomach goes woozy.

Shout, "You gotta pick me!" when team captains get choosy.

Rescue your friend from The Bully. Then hide.

Upset the whole team when your goal shot goes wide.

Lose the match when your Four-Square ball bounces away.

End up out of the game when you're aching to play.

Still—100 %—recess rules every day!

Wet Play
Fi Calvert

"Wet play!" The teachers say.
Everybody shouts "Hooray!"
"Games out! Let's not shout!
Tommy, please don't run about!"

Hatty builds a Lego tower,
Ashton colours in a flower.
Fern and Krishna play Top Trumps,
Lottie's on a chair, then …
JUMPS!

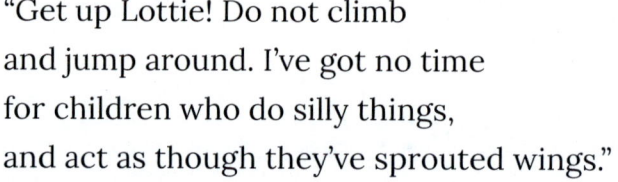

"Get up Lottie! Do not climb
and jump around. I've got no time
for children who do silly things,
and act as though they've sprouted wings."

Lottie settles down to draw,
Lou is rolling on the floor.
Tommy (who's still running round)
trips on Lou and hits the ground.

"What on earth is going on?
Playtime's not five minutes gone.
Settle down now, please just play
quiet as mice or - games away!"

Every child's now on a chair,
Benji's styling Harvey's hair
(not with gel - he's using glue!)
Abigail has lost a shoe.

"Harvey, what's that in your hair?
Really kids! I do despair!
Hang on Abi, where's your shoe?
Children this is like a zoo!"

BRRRIIIIIINNNNG!

"Oh! Thank goodness- there's the bell!
This wet play has not gone well.
I think a book, now, would be best.
After that we need a rest!"

Sonnet Moon
Debra Bertulis

Moon plays Mozart on Spring evenings
Feather-like notes
Tap at my window
Stirring my soul
Soothing my mind

Moon sings the blues on warm Summer nights
Sweet notes woven like gossamer
Creep through my window
Lull me to slumber
Until morning

Moon reads Kipling on crisp Autumn evenings
Whispers of roads forgotten
But alive still
Brush at my window
Hush me to sleep

Moon reads Shakespeare on Winter nights
Sonnets of love
Of passion
Pirouette at my window and
Capture my heart.

Sia Jumping
Chrissie Gittins

Sia jumps off the window sill
into her grandfather's arms
and the red tree jumps with her.

Grandfather stands further away.

Sia jumps off the window sill
into her grandfather's arms
and the rain jumps with her.

Grandfather stands further away.

Sia jumps off the window sill
into her grandfather's arms
and the lightening sky jumps with her.

The rain drops stop, the leaves fall
and the sun comes shining through.

Shell
Paula Thompson

I found you,
half-hidden,
on the beach.
Buried in sand
no wave could reach.
I turned you over,
inspected your twists.
Traced your spirals,
curled you up in my fist.
Inside: smooth and pale,
fragile and pearly
as a fingernail.
A vacant bauble –
a home no more.
My very own piece
of the ocean floor.
I found you,
empty.
But you spoke to me:
a rushing whooshing
song of the sea.
I found you,
abandoned on the sand.
I'll keep you.
A shoreline treasure
in the palm of my hand.

Sandy Days
Clara McShane

Easter eggs in craggy pocks
Muckross beach drive, skimming rocks
daisy chains tied up with grass
hiding from being brought to mass
ice pop melting down my palm
cattle lowing, baby lamb
cousins, family, dad is home
chasing waves and dodging foam
glass bottles of 7-up
jellies in a paper cup
getting late for sleepy head
carried safely straight to bed
cloudless nights and starry plough
moonlight 'pon my little brow
back to Dublin, tear-filled car
knowing home is not that far.

Mermaid
Sarah Wallis

untended, abandoned but moored
to a tree, is Mermaid, a once proud sailboat
becalmed in the forest, brambled

to beehive, hosting nest lichen, mushroom
and aviary, stuck on her high keel, deep
in the rich loam and dreaming of the glittering,

mermaiding bright silver blue sea, her once sunlit
sails, yellow spinnaker in full wind pocket
splendour, hands to the mast, halyards rattling,

chasing down dolphins nosing her bow wave...

                              like a fairy tale ended,

a mermaid once landed is not free, and nor is a boat

that's tasted saltwater, wind-chastened,
out of her element, greening
in ivy abandon, and losing herself to a tree.

Bedtime
Coral Rumble

Fishing boats line up on shore -
They've done so many times before -
Weathered by the sea and sand,
Calmly resting on the land.

Nets are drying, oars are still,
The evening sunshine starts to spill
Over the sides of paint-cracked hulls
That sigh beneath the circling gulls.

Gentle ripples stroke their sterns
As evening sets the tide to turn,
And, in the glow of harbour lights,
They close their eyes and say goodnight.

Help Line
Brian Mackenwells

So
it's like this:
My show builds up
to this trick where
I pull a rabbit out of my hat.
Sorry, yes, I did forget to mention that I'm a magician.
Anyway, the rabbit.
Ta-dah!
But then we see
the rabbit has its own little hat
and he pulls from it
a hare.
The hare, you see
also has a slightly bigger hat –
Sorry, yes, I am getting to why I called you –
So the hare pulls out of its hat
a Labrador!
And then I come out
of the Labrador's hat.
Thank you, it is quite hard to do.
But today
it went wrong.

The Labrador was wearing a hat
I had never seen before
and instead of me,
he pulled out a tiger
which, fair play to the Labrador,
I'm not sure how he did it
or where he found this tiger.
But see,
the tiger
was also wearing a hat
and she pulled a polar bear from hers.
At this point
the stage was getting a bit crowded.
And it didn't stop there.

You can probably see why I'm calling you.

So, could you tell me
if you take strays
at your whale sanctuary?

Elliot's Laces
Elenore Byrne

Elliot's laces are slippery strings
that refuse to stay taut on his shoe.
At first they look right when he tugs the loops tight
then they wriggle and slowly undo.

Laces a flap he meanders and skips,
but Elliot won't trip or fall.
His talent is dodging the laces dislodging.
Untied makes no difference at all.

Fun Friday
Fiona Halliday

Freddy Frog likes fresh froggy fries on Friday,
With frosted fruitcake and fruity frog-shakes,
Freddy Frog finds friends to eat French food with,
Freddy's friends feel he's froggy-fantastic!
Fabulous Freddy Frog's the friendliest frog in Frogdom!

I Cry
Jonathan Sellars

I cry for no reason, no reason at all,
I cry when I'm hurt after taking a fall,
I cry when I stub all my toes on the bin,
I cry when I lose, I cry when I win,
I cry when I'm sad, I cry when I laugh,
I cry in my bed and I cry in the bath.
Some days I cry lots, some days I just don't,
Some days I admit it, some days I just won't.
It's healthy to cry, but I think it's worth stating,
Crying this much can be so dehydrating.

Secret Toenail Clipper
Alex Price

There's a secret toenail clipper
Who sneaks in my room at night
They clip off all my toenails
Then they disappear from sight

I made a plan to catch them
Putting traps around my bed
But the toenail clipper got away
I caught my mum instead

A Rainy Day
Rhiannon Oliver

What to do with a rainy day?
Stay in the house and hide away?

No! Pop on some wellies and zip up your jacket,
Put some snacks in a waterproof packet
And head out into the rainy weather -
The rain wants to have some fun together!

Say "Hello" to the rain, say "So nice to meet you!"
Let the rain know that she's totally free to
Land on your face, your elbows, your tum,
Hold out your hands and stick out your tongue.

Dance as she falls and waters the world,
Spin all around, twist, whirl and twirl.
And this bit's important, don't get in a muddle -
You must go and seek out a gigantic puddle...

Because jumping in puddles is a gift from the rain!
Land with a splash and then do it again.
Splooshing and sploshing and thudding about
Is the best fun ever, of that there's no doubt.

And please, don't be scared of getting quite wet,
You've been wet in the bath before, I bet.

Storm Coming
Gillian Spiller

Everybody's looking at the cloudless sky
The boats on the stream go floating by
The kids at the park are having fun
Enjoy the lovely weather, everyone!

Everybody's looking at the cloudy sky
People take in clothes that are nearly dry
No-one wants to play in the park – no sun!
Keep an eye on the weather, everyone!

Everybody's looking at the stormy sky
The clouds, now dark and thick all start to fly
Enormous plopping raindrops, one by one
Get inside quickly, everyone!

Everybody's looking at the scary sky
Nobody is playing and we all know why
Thunder shakes the house as the lightning comes
Stay inside and stay safe everyone!

Window Holiday
Catherine Olver

one breakfast I spill milk across the sky

two creamy calves stick out their tongues to slurp it up
from cirrostratus grass   and on the clouds' low slopes
a wisping steam train slowly lugs three carriages
of daffodils   and insubstantial hopes

a pod of purple porpoises starts playing in my street
they hide-and-seek in nimbostratus foam
droplets from their blowholes   spot the window glass
they mock me   stuck inside   and stuck at home

lumpy grey   grumpily   thumping   a rumpus of elephants
fling my nimbusnimble little brother from their backs
as he falls   I catch him   as he crashes haul him in
splendorous splashes drench our chilly skin

then the evening phoenix   in a flare of flames proclaims
the dragons are coming   the dragons are dipping
to sip the sinking sun   yes the dragons have come
to spit *F*I*R*E*W*O*R*K*S*

when did my disappointments disappear?

never mind the planes   and where they go
imagination   and the wind   can blow
a window holiday   right here

At Sunrise
Kathryn Dove

A blackbird fidgets on the fence
like a black suited commuter
impatient for the first bus.

The flat clouds glint orange
like brand new pennies, spilling
into the till, ready for change.

The apple tree sways
like a dancer limbering up
for the gala opening.

The sun makes its appearance
like a movie star emerging
from a dark limousine to flash
a golden smile upon the waiting world.

Balloons on Sticks at Parties: why we are all a bit cross
Lesley James

We walked into my birthday party
Like we were walking onto a yacht* (* song by Carly Simon)
Until we saw a ghastly sight
That made us all want to walk out:

THE BALLOONS WERE ALL TIED TO STICKS!
WHAAAT?!

Balloons: where's all your bimbling?
You should be bobbing about
You shouldn't be tethered to a soldierly stick
Like a lollipop - it makes me want to shout:

YOU ALL LOOK PETRIFIED. YOU'VE BEEN TIED TO THE STAKE.
LITERALLY.

Balloons should always be on the verge of escape
for every second you see them
A string is the only thin tether they need
Balloons should invite you to free them

OR POP THEM IN THE MADNESS OF UTTER PARTY GLEE.

The very point about balloons is that they bobble about
They vacillate hesitantly
The very best thing about a balloon
Is the bumbling, the nearly-free jeopardy

WE LOVE THEIR WILL-THEY-WON'T-THEY WOBBLE,
LIKE JELLYFISH IN THE OCEAN.

So who did this crime? C'mon. Fess up.
Who stopped the balloons from giggling?
Who trussed 'em like turkeys?
Who stopped them from wobbling?

- OH. HI MUM. NICE PARTY. YES, LOVELY, THANK YOU.
 YEAH, I LOVE ALL THE BALLOONS -
NICE TOUCH

The Magic
Lisa Varchol Perron

I am the magic that swirls in the night,
the shape of a shadow that slinks out of sight,
the trouble that bubbles and builds to a boil,
the steam as it creeps in a slithering coil.

I am the creak of the branches that sway,
the nudge of a breeze as it tugs you away,
the circle of moonlight alone in the sky,
the faraway howl, the footsteps nearby.

I am the tiniest tickle of fear,
the wisp of a whisper that itches your ear,
the goosebump, the shiver, the chill in the air,
the whiff of adventure, the taste of a dare.

I am the darkness in which you delight.
I am the magic of Halloween night!

I Wish

Tom Moody

I wish I was as smart as him.
I wish I was as cool.
I wish I was as popular
with all the kids at school.

I wish I had as many friends.
I wish I was as tall.
I wish, like him, I was the brightest
kid to walk the halls.

I wish I was as rich as him.
I wish my clothes were new.
I wish my teeth were straight like his.
I wish I had a clue.

But I am not the kid he is.
I know I'll never be.
I could never be like him.
Instead, I'll be like me.

Advice for Meeting a Yeti
Coral Rumble

If you ever see a Yeti
Stare hard, because I bet he
Will quickly try to hide behind a tree,

And when he's still and hiding,
Don't expect him to come striding
Out to shake your hand or come to tea.

For a Yeti likes his space
And will never show his face,
So turn around and simply let him be.

He is big and he is hairy
But that doesn't make him scary,
Above all, a Yeti just wants to be free.

His abominable face
Will disappear, without a trace,
If you just tiptoe along, real quietly.

A Hug for your Head
Carl Burkitt

A woolly hat is a hug for your head.
It's a glove for your skull,
fluffy wallpaper for your brain.

A woolly hat is the opposite of snow.
It's a summer's glow,
a campfire's flame.

A woolly hat is a chili pepper for hair.
It's a roast dinner with a bobble,
a hot chocolate in Spain.

A woolly hat is a duvet on a hike.
It's a warm bath on your bike,
a friend in the rain.

Magic in the Air
Elisabeth Kelly

I can breathe fire,
well smoke,
sort of.

It happens in the cold,

I blow and blow,
the air changes
right in front of my face.

Perhaps,
I am a dragon.

One day my wings may grow,
I will swoop and soar over shimmering hills,
glide over glistening glens,
frost on my claws.

My Dad,
can do it too.

Maybe we are all dragons?
We just forgot.

Wintertime Fair
Mary E. Cronin

The setting sun shimmers a silvery pink,
casting a glow on the ice skating rink.
Skaters go 'round, some wobbly, some steady.
Snowflakes float past like party confetti.

Shoppers choose gifts of candy and toys.
Giggles and jingle bells add to the noise.
Mountains of pretzels and apples for sale
by a gingerbread cottage—follow the trail.

Parents sip cups of hot coffee or cider,
wrapping their woolly scarves tighter and tighter.
Donuts with sprinkles and cocoa with cream,
colored lights twinkle – a fairy tale dream.

Laughter and singing fill the town square.
So much to explore at the wintertime fair!

Winter Fairies
Moe Phillips

Outside my window, a howling wind grows near
Wild Storm Fairies are dancing through the atmosphere
Frosting the mountain forest, freezing the deep lake,
pulling cold on their sleds, leaving winter in their wake

Fairies make a fury of the elements they rule
flying from the frozen north, using star dust for their fuel
Above, the winter skies are ablaze with northern lights,
a cosmic show of color, created by the sprites

They laugh and chase each other through the icy air,
with bright scarlet cheeks and snowflakes in their hair
A blizzard is their breakfast, a hailstorm late-day tea
Fairies whistle up a wind that freezes every tree

One morning without warning, the imps stop in their tracks
On this day the Star of Dawn feels warm upon their backs

Once again, the Earth has turned her face up to the Sun,
robins sing out to Fairies, 'Your winter work is done!'

Christmas Sounds
Carole Bromley

Bell tinkle,
tree twinkle
parcel thud in hall
wrapping rustle
shopping bustle
whispery snow flake fall

carol singers
bell ringers
fires that crack and spark
pud stirrers
mixer whirrers
stockings in the dark

late shoppers
cork poppers
paper ripping joy
wish bone snappers
joke unwrappers
giddy girls and boys

heel dragging
kids lagging
Mum, it's Christmas Day!
then mince-pie munch
and fruit cake crunch
and hours and hours to play.

The Snowman's List

Julie Anna Douglas

Lend me your hat and long, stripy scarf
just in case it snows.
Fetch two chunks of coal for eyes
and a carrot for my nose.
Arrange some pebbles in a curve
to let me smile all day.
You can have them back again
when I melt away.

Home Sweet Home
Nannie Shakespeare

Biting winds and frost bite toes,
Glowing cheeks and tingling nose,
Roaring fire and blanket soft,
Cosy cottage, stony croft,
Gathered with your family dear,
Sharing each and every fear,
Love and comfort, hope and cheer,
Home sweet home, all through the year.

The Gift

Helen Dineen

If I could travel round the world in eighty years or more,
I'd seek out special memories and bring them to your door,

A trek across a mountain range with peaks of crisp, white snow,
A paddle through the tropics where the twisted mangroves grow,

A flight above the desert in a grand hot air balloon,
A swim in placid rivers, lit up by the harvest moon,

A chase across a cloudless sky, to catch the northern lights,
A foray to a lake to see flamingos in full flight,

A ride through steep-cut canyons on a horse that's proud and strong,
A dive to precious coral reefs, where bright fish dart along,

A taxi through each city, full of hustle, smells and din,
A meal with each community that welcomes strangers in,

If I could travel round the world in eighty years, it's true,
I'd pack up all those memories and bring the world to you,

I'd say, "Let's stick the kettle on, we'll have a cup of tea,"
And then we'd both go travelling, by land and air and sea,

Yes, we would both go travelling –
                        On clouds of memories.